I'M TOO OLD

CARY HOLBERT

ISBN-13: 978-0615890098
ISBN-10: 0615890091

Introduction

The Dirty Feet Ministries Bible Studies Series is designed to encourage you to reflect honestly on your life and then make adjustments to improve areas you identify as missing the mark of Jesus. The study is a collection of six actual events, with fictitious names given to the characters, followed by a Bible passage and then probing questions.

Dirty Feet Ministries believes the Word of God is the final rule for faith and life. In other words, all we need to know about God and to live for God is in the Bible. The real life events are given as examples of what life looks like when a person says yes to Jesus Christ and His will, or, in some cases, rebels against Him. The Word of God is given not just to read or develop a theology of words but to reveal God so that we might know Him and enjoy Him.

In an era when tenure, generational employment, and pensions are being wiped out and replaced with 401Ks, our God has not wavered in His call on His people's lives regardless of age. Your worth and value are defined by the blood of Christ. Your call is to pick up the banner of Christ and march as a soldier until you have breathed your last in this life. This study is about such an event. While the world may discard you, God never will and in your weakness, God will manifest His presence.

The Architect of the universe and Creator of all things is saying, Come to me and I will enable you to love, live, and enjoy life to the fullest. In our broken world, it is time for those who know God to fine-tune our lives for Him, and for those who don't, to turn to Him.

Table of Contents

The Event

It's the early 90s and the local church has had its annual mission conference, fanning the flame for making Christ known to the nations. This included not only supporting missionaries financially but also participating through sending members of the local church on short-term, cross-cultural mission opportunities. This short-term trip served two purposes; first by actually making Christ known cross culturally and, second, it gave people an opportunity to test out their potential calling to fulltime missionary service. The buzz of the opportunity stirred a lot of interest. The project included working with a local church in a foreign country and building a home in two weeks for a family who was living literally in a cardboard house. The local church provided the spiritual nourishment and the mission team provided the physical needs under the banner of Jesus Christ.

Who can go? Building a house in two weeks

requires the lifting of cinder blocks, mortar, fabricated roofing, rebar, and raking, and smoothing concrete in 100-degree heat, with a hole in the ground for the toilet. This was not going to be a vacation or a glamorous environment. As you might think, most of those who were in their 70s and upwards didn't see themselves as candidates. They thought this adventure was for young people. However, there was an exception; Ms. M., who, for some reason, God stirred and did not leave alone until she said 'yes.' Ms. M. was in her 70s and ready to work for the Lord.

The team of about 25 ranged in age from 7 years old to 70 plus. You can see the wheels turning as people are trying to think what can a 70-year-old or a 7-year-old do in this kind of environment. The team arrived safely after a 6-hour plane flight and a 6-hour drive, wearing their mission t-shirts. The project coordinators spent the first evening planning and getting assignments for the team.

The work began and it took everyone working 9 hours a day to stay on schedule. It was an interesting environment at the work site. An old water tanker pumped water into an old steel drum in front of the work site. It was blistering hot and the foul smell of that pumped water made you nauseas. It was inconceivable that families would cook or drink that water, even if was boiled first.

The team did use the water to clean their tools at the end of the day. One of the team members had a habit of chewing his finger nails and after the third day of work, he forgot about the water. The result was he spent several days on the hole-in-the-ground toilet facility. This 30+ year old was important to the manual labor of the work. However, Ms. M was able to help pick up another person's duties so the work could stay on schedule. The 7-year-old helped as well by taking refreshments to team members. The two weeks came to a close and the house was completed on schedule. It was an amazing event as the family, which now had electricity and a cinder block house, joined hands and gave thanks with the team for all He, Jesus Christ, had done.

Lesson I

What is the age limit on Christian Service?

For the Christian, as long as you have breath, you're to be an active servant of the Lord.

The event

1. What age limit do you think should be set before you allow people to serve?

2. What happens when you tell a segment of the Christian community their services are no longer needed?

3. How would Ms. M been impacted if she was told she was too old to go on this mission trip?

4. What do you think a 7-year-old was able to accomplish?

5. What happened to the 30-year-old?

6. What kind of impact do you think the diversity in age had on the family the house was being built for?

The Bible Passage
Luke 1:41-45, 2 Kings 11:21, Matthew 4:21, Revelation 1:9-11, 1 Timothy 4:11-16.

You are born to serve God.

1. Luke 1:41-45
   a. How old was the child when he first made Christ known to his mother?

2. 2 Kings 11:21
   a. How old was this person when he became King of Judah?

3. Matthew 4:21, Revelation 1:9-11
   a. John the Apostle was between 13 to 18 when Jesus called him to be an apostle and then he wrote the Book of Revelation, which is dated about 95AD. What is the approximate age of the Apostle John then in 95 AD?

4. Revelation 1:11

    a. What does God have John do at this age?

5. 1 Timothy 4:11-16

    a. What encouragement does Paul give
    Timothy?

Remember:

    1. There is no age limit on Christian service.

    2. You are born again to serve God.

Lesson II

Who should be on the team?

If I chose then it will never be any better than me.

The event

1. What is the goal of the mission?

2. Who calls Mrs. M to go?

3. Who was the house being built for?

4. What happens if the task at hand is the focus instead of the mission?

5. In whose name did the team go under? Then who is in charge of seeing the task is completed?

The Bible Passage
Matthew 16:18, Luke 6:12-16, Matthew 9:9, 1 Peter 2:4-6

God is on a building campaign that the faithfulness and power of His Word ensure its perfect completion.

1. Luke 6:12-16
   a. Who chose the Apostles?

2. Matthew 9:9
   a. What did Matthew do for a living? What experience did he have as an apostle?

3. Matthew 16:18

    a. Who is going to build the church?

4. 1 Peter 2:4-6

    a. How are believers described?

5. 1 Peter 2:4-6

    a. Who is placing each stone?

6. 1 Peter 2:4-6

    a. What do we offer?

Remember:

    1. Jesus Christ is building His church and it will be completed.

    2. Your life is to be lived as an offering to God.

Lesson III

I am willing. Send me

Are you willing?

The event

1. Who was willing?

2. Does that mean everyone who says 'I am willing' should be sent? Why or why not?

3. How does a 7-year-old say, 'I am willing'?

4. Why is it important to encourage those who desire to serve the Lord?

5. How does Ms. M's willingness, and then follow-through, affect those in her age group in the local church?

The Bible Passage
Isaiah 6:8, Ezekiel 3:16-27, Romans 10:14-15, Matthew 25:34-36, Matthew 28:19

To go is what God desires.

1. Isaiah 6:8
   a. What does the Lord ask, and who responds?

2. Romans 10:14-15
   a. How do they hear?

3. Ezekiel 3:16-17
   a. How did God communicate with His people?

What is the consequence if the watchman fails to do what God says?

4. Matthew 25:34-36

    a. What are works that glorify God?

5. Matthew 28:19

    a. What are we told to do?

Remember:

    1. The church is on the offense and commanded to go with the gospel.

    2. We are to communicate the gospel verbally and by our actions in caring for the needs of others.

Lesson IV

Not what you think

God's ways are God events.

The event

1. What kind of house did the family live in?

2. When is the last time a tanker unloaded your drinking water in a steel drum in your front yard?

3. When is the last time you saw a house built in two weeks?

4. When is the last time you passed a construction site with a 7-year-old and 70+ year old working?

5. How long did it take them to get to the work site?

The Bible Passage
1 Kings 17:7-16

God's way of doing things leaves no doubt to the recipient who it is from.

1. 1 Kings 17:7-9
    a. What is the present situation in the land and who does God send Elijah to for help? Why her?

2. 1 Kings 17:10-12

    a. What was the widow doing when Elijah arrived?

    b. What had she and her son planned to do? If you were Elijah, what would you have expected?

3. 1 King 17:13, 14

    a. What did Elijah instruct her to do?

4. 1 Kings 17:15

    a. What would you have done? What did she do?

5. 1 Kings 17:16

    a. Did God provide for them all?

Remember:

1. God works in mysterious ways so if you let the world dictate the way God works, you will miss God working.

2. As we trust God and act in accordance with His will, our life will have an eternal impact on others.

Lesson V

The ordinary become extraordinary

The plain gives room for God's glory.

The event

1. How do you get 25 people to volunteer to travel 6 hours in a plane and 6 hours in a van to work in 100-degree heat to build a house for someone they don't know and will probably never see again in this life?

2. What happened to the 30-year-old?

3. How did the team make up for the loss of a key worker?

4. How is it that two cultures, the local church, and foreign missionaries are able to work together to accomplish one goal, and that is to make Christ known?

5. How do you get 25 people, most of whom have no construction experience, to unite and do that which is not ordinary work for them?

The Bible Passage
Acts 8:1-4

The ordinary is empowered to be extraordinary.

1. Acts 8:1a

a. What was Saul doing?

2. Acts 8:1b

   a. Who was run out of town, why, and where?

3. Acts 8:2

   a. Who stepped up and buried Stephen in the midst of the hostility?

4. Acts 8:3

   a. How fierce was the persecution?

5. Acts 8:4

   a. Would you describe these ordinary people as refugees or missionaries? Why or why not?

6. Acts 8:4

    a. What did they do when run out of town?

Remember:

    1. God chooses the ordinary to manifest His glory.

    2. You can do extraordinary things because God will enable you.

Lesson VI

Job well done

Who wants to hear the words, 'You did an okay job'?

The event

1. How important was it that the house was completed?

2. Do you think the trip accomplished its purposes?

3. What effect do you think the success of the team had on the church that sent them?

4. What impact do you think this trip had on each team member?

5. What ancillary impact do you think seeing the t-shirts and reading the mission's literature had on the people on the plane, in the airport, the border and custom border agents?

The Bible Passage
Luke 9:57-62

The focus is Godward, the work is of the Kingdom, and the call is to excellence.

1. Luke 9:57-58
    a. What can someone expect who follows Jesus?

2. Luke 9:59
    a. What do you think about the man's request?

3. Luke 9:59-60

    a. How would you have responded to Jesus? How important is the gospel message?

4. Luke 9:61

    a. What do you think about this request?

5. Luke 9:62

    a. What is expected of a disciple of Jesus?

Remember:

    1. Disciples of Christ are called to be single-minded in their pursuit of Jesus.

    2. The work of the Kingdom of God is not without cost.

3. The beauty of the gospel is while we work, we also rest in what Jesus Christ has done. We are safe and secure in Jesus.

Lesson VII

To God be the glory

Does the light shine on me or on the Lord Jesus Christ?

The event

1. Who called the team to go?

2. Who called each individual to go?

3. Who provided all the resources necessary to complete the task?

4. Who provided travel mercies and wisdom to

complete the task?

5. Who picked the family and founded the church in the foreign country?

6. Who was given the glory?

The Bible Passage
1 Corinthians 10:28-33

What thrills me? Is it me?

1. 1 Corinthians 10:28-30
    a. How is the person's freedom to be conducted?

2. 1 Corinthians 10:31
    a. While the inference is to eating and drinking, to what else does this apply?

3. 1 Corinthians 10:31

    a. What should every activity of our life do?

4. 1 Corinthians 10:32-33

    a. What are some possible cultural differences that may exist between Jew and Gentile?

5. 1 Corinthians 10:33

    a. What is Paul's goal in the way he lives?

Remember:

1. Your entire life should be lived in such a way that God is being honored.

2. Your life is missional.

Lesson VIII

What now?

Many folks will finish what they're doing, wash their hands then move on to the next life event. This pattern repeats itself in the Christian community as well. You spend six to eight weeks reading, fellowshipping, praying, and completing exercises only to move on to the next event in your life. Often our faith is not more than an inch deep and nothing more than hot air. We are robbed and rob others of all that God wants for humanity.

Mrs. M could have said no to God's call, saying she was too old, and people would have encouraged that decision. Maybe you are in a similar situation but it is not age – it is that you have children or feel some other sort of inadequacy. In your weakness is when God shines and your work becomes a work for His glory. The mission trip was a work for His glory that was taxing and demanding. The Lord makes that clear right up front: this call to Kingdom work is demanding and once started, it is to be finished.

Don't sit on the sidelines any longer. Step up and join in the only enterprise that will truly be successful and last forever.

Author Biography

Cary Holbert is a pastor, public speaker, author, and financial and management advocate. As a public speaker, Pastor Cary has specialized in vision casting for over 25 years. Pastor Cary has successfully helped both non-profit and for-profit organizations in financial and management aspects of their business. With a Master's degree in Pastoral Leadership from the Columbia Biblical Seminary, Pastor Cary serves on the board of the Garden Worship Center and is also the President of the Dirty Feet Ministries, which writes and publishes ministry training literature, including *The Elder Handbook, Part I & II*, and *The Dirty Feet Ministries Small Group Bible Study Six Part Series*.

<u>Books by Dirty Feet Ministries, Inc</u>

<u>Small Group Bible Study:</u>

The Lady Who Couldn't See
I'm Too Old
The Dad Who Left Me
Why Give Money?
I've Tried Everything, Except
Who is Your Timothy or Lydia?

Leadership Training:

The Elder
The Elder in Action
The Deacon

The Servant Series:

1 Peter

Our Website:
http://www.christianbooksbible.org/

Our email:
christianbiblebooks@sc.rr.com